THE HEYDAY OF THE HST

Ian Allan
PUBLISHING

GAVIN MORRISON

Front cover: Dundee and the Tay bridge stand out clearly on a superb summer's day — 22 June 1989 — as the 10.30 from King's Cross–Aberdeen approaches Wormit with power car No 43094, in InterCity 'swallow' livery, bringing up the rear. *Gavin Morrison*

Back cover: At 13.59 on 1 June 2002 a pair of Midland Mainline HSTs in that operator's original style of livery pass at Lenton West Junction, Nottingham, with trains to and from St Pancras. The power cars nearer the camera are No 43059 on the down train and No 43076 on the up working. *Gavin Morrison*

Previous page: HST services on the East Coast main line were introduced between May 1978 and May 1979. The 11.00 King's Cross–Edinburgh is shown crossing Selby swing bridge on 22 September 1983, just before services were re-routed via the new Selby diversion, which opened officially on 24 September 1983. The rear power car is No 43043, which entered service in January 1978 and was allocated to Heaton as part of set No 254 021; the set number can just be discerned. Named *Leicestershire County Cricket Club* on 19 May 1997, No 43043 has worked services on the Midland main line since 1988 and is one of 25 HST power cars currently fitted with a Paxman 12VP185 engine. *Gavin Morrison*

First published 2007

ISBN (10) 0 7110 3184 3
ISBN (13) 978 0 7110 3184 5

© Ian Allan Publishing 2007

Published by Ian Allan Publishing

an imprint of Ian Allan Publishing Ltd, Hersham, Surrey KT12 4RG.
Printed by Ian Allan Printing Ltd, Hersham, Surrey KT12 4RG.

Code: 0704/B1

Visit the Ian Allan Publishing web site at:
www.ianallanpublishing.com

Introduction

I am delighted to have been given the opportunity to present a colour album on the High Speed Train (HST). Whilst the early BR liveries were impressive, the wide variety of colour schemes introduced by the privatised Train Operating Companies (TOCs) has been nothing short of spectacular.

It is hard to believe that the HST was conceived by BR as a temporary measure pending electrification and the introduction of the Advanced Passenger Train (APT). Sanctioned in 1970, the project progressed with remarkable speed, the prototype being completed within two years, the aim being to have trains in service by 1975.

In order to achieve the desired 125mph top speed a power unit of arounf 4,500hp was considered necessary, but there was also a need to keep weight to a minimum, and no suitable unit was available. Accordingly it was decided that the High Speed Diesel Train (as it was then known) should be operated as a push-pull set, with two power cars, one at either end, each with a Paxman Valenta engine of 2,250hp.

Difficulties were experienced in obtaining agreement of terms from the unions to drive the trains, which curtailed some test running, but eventually, on 2 August 1973, only three years from being sanctioned, the prototype left King's Cross for Newcastle with a press run, and guests were treated to 125mph running on the British Rail network for the first time. The trip was a resounding success and received much praise from all on board. The success of the project may have been due to the building of the prototype and the extensive testing involved; in fact by May 1974 the set had covered no less than 100,000 miles.

The prototype entered public service on 5 May 1975 working services between Bristol and Paddington, and, although maximum speed was restricted to 100mph, passengers were apparently so keen to travel on it that many were altering their journey times to fit in with its diagrams. By now the production of the power cars and Mk 3 coaches was progressing quickly, the former to a modified (and much more pleasing) design which looks as modern today as it did 30 years ago.

The prototype claimed the world speed record for diesel traction of 143mph near Thirsk on the East Coast main line on 11 June 1974, and indeed there are tales of drivers getting very close to 140mph on the Western Region main line with passenger trains until governors were fitted, allowing a maximum of 128mph when power is now cut off. Not only was the speed performance entirely new for the railways, but the braking capabilities were remarkable: stopping from 125mph was achieved in 1,930 yards, whereas a locomotive would take 2,200 yards from 100mph. The performance of the train revolutionised the timetables, although

Left: No 43086 brings up the rear of the 06.45 Newcastle–Plymouth approaching Burton-upon-Trent on 6 April 2002. Delivered new on 19 April 1978 as part of set No 254 016, it went first to Heaton and then on to Craigentinny a few months later, when the full HST service to/from Edinburgh was introduced on the East Coast main line. Displaced from CrossCountry duties, to which it had been cascaded following ECML electrification, by 'Voyagers', it passed to Midland Mainline for 'Project Rio' duties between St Pancras and Manchester, being named *Rio Talisman*. *Gavin Morrison*

Above: The cooling towers of Drax power station send clouds high into the sky above an unidentified HST forming a northbound express, which was probably heading for Inverness or Aberdeen. It is seen racing past Burn on the Selby diversion on 28 November 1996. *Gavin Morrison*

there were for several years only a few lines where the trains' full potential could be realised; even today they are restricted on the Midland main line to a maximum of 110mph.

The trains have enjoyed on the whole a good reliability record, although the very hot summer of 1983 led to considerable problems with overheating engines, which caused disruption to services. Much time and effort was spent by BR and Paxman in resolving this problem, but even today very hot weather can still occasionally cause trouble.

The total mileage covered by the HSTs is around 1,000 million, a staggering figure that must surely constitute a world record. Equally remarkable is that until 1997 — 21 years after the trains' introduction — no passengers were killed while travelling on an HST. Since then there have been three major disasters involving

loss of life, none of which were attributable to the trains; indeed, given the severity of the accidents, it is a miracle that the figures were so low. Probably the worst fault afflicting an HST occurred near Northallerton in August 1979, when a gearbox seized at 70mph and derailed the train, fortunately without serious consequences.

The HSTs have now been around for more than 30 years; normally this would be sufficient to encompass the complete history of a class, but such is far from the case here. A major refurbishment programme that will involve the majority of the sets is currently in hand, and the power cars are receiving new engines supplied by MTU, which will probably extend their life by 10 years. I doubt if there is any other rail network in the world investing so heavily in 30-year-old trains to allow them to continue on the top-link main-line work for which they were built. It is food for thought that the 'Deltics' lasted 20 years, the 'Westerns' 16; even Gresley's famous

'A4' Pacifics managed only around 26 years. Some, like the surviving Class 47s, have put in 40 years, but such locomotives are no longer employed on main-line diagrams on a daily basis.

This album is intended as a purely photographic record; for those readers interested in technical information and details of the various carriages I would strongly recommend *HST Silver Jubilee* and *The Power of the HSTs*, from which much of the information contained in the captions has been obtained.

No doubt the HSTs will receive many new liveries in the years to come, justifying a second volume on these remarkable trains.

Gavin Morrison
Mirfield
February 2007

Bibliography
The Allocation History of the BR Diesels and Electrics (Part 2) by Roger Harris (published by the author in 2002)
HST Silver Jubilee by Colin J. Marsden (Ian Allan Publishing, 2001)
The Power of the HSTs by Colin J. Marsden (OPC, 2006)

Left: Entering traffic in May 1979, power car No 43119 was initially part of the last set (No 254 032) allocated to services on the East Coast main line. In 2007, named *Harrogate Spa*, it is still working on the ECML for Great North Eastern Railway (GNER) on services not covered by Class 91 electrics. It is seen here on 14 February 1997 passing through Northallerton at around 125mph at the head of the up 'Highland Chieftain' (07.50 Inverness–King's Cross) in GNER livery but with coaches still in InterCity livery. *Gavin Morrison*

Right: Early in 2003 Midland Mainline decided to replace its attractive turquoise, orange and grey livery with this dark blue with white flashes. No 43166 was one of the first HST power cars to receive the new scheme and is shown at Neville Hill depot, Leeds, on 2 March 2003 just before entering service; note that it has still to receive its number. It first entered traffic at Plymouth Laira in September 1981 and has changed operators several times and worn many liveries. Most Midland Mainline power cars are owned by Porterbrook Leasing, but No 43166 is one of the minority that belong to Angel Trains. *Gavin Morrison*

In the latter years of BR, power cars — mainly those allocated to Neville Hill shed at Leeds — received a variety of different-sized numerals, a selection of which are shown here.

Left: No 43118 with small numbers and No 43074 with the correct size at King's Cross, 18 March 1989. *Gavin Morrison*

Centre left: Another variation: No 43123 — one of the eight buffer-fitted power cars — with black numbers on a full yellow front end, compares with No 43077, with standard numbers, at King's Cross on 28 March 1989. *Gavin Morrison*

Below left: Large numbers on No 43155 passing the sea wall at Dawlish on 25 August 1990. *Gavin Morrison*

Below: No 43098 displays only the last two digits of its number as it rounds the curve at Whitehall Junction, Leeds, on 2 October 1991. *Gavin Morrison*

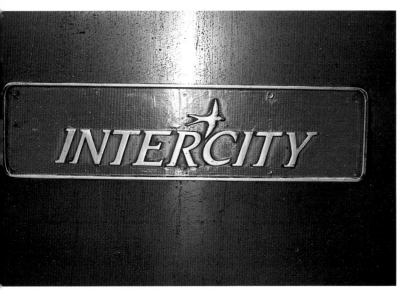

Selection of names
Above: No 43154

Below: No 43072

Above: No 43158

Below: No 43170

Above: During August 1975 the prototype High Speed Diesel Train (HSDT) set, No 252 001, was released from its duties on the Western Region to take part in the Stockton & Darlington 150 celebrations, being exhibited at BREL Shildon Works alongside many famous locomotives. Few attending the exhibition can have realised that this unit would have more impact on the railways than had most of the other exhibits in the past. *Gavin Morrison*

Below left: The climax of the Stockton & Darlington 150 extravaganza was on the August bank holiday, when an incredible procession of steam motive power made its way from Shildon to Darlington, with the HSDT (exhibit 34) bringing up the rear. Thousands of people turned out to witness at close quarters a spectacle that is unlikely ever to be repeated. *Gavin Morrison*

On 19 March 1978 a remarkable event was staged at the north end of York station using the Scarborough through and bay platforms for a special filming showing the development of the East Coast main line motive power over the years. Included in the line-up were Stirling Single No 1 and Ivatt Atlantic No 251, both from the Great Northern Railway, North Eastern Worsdell 4-4-0 No 1621, Gresley LNER Class A4 Pacific No 4468 *Mallard*, 'Deltic' No 55 013 *The Black Watch* and HST unit No 254 009. *Gavin Morrison*

Below: A line-up of HSTs has been an everyday sight at Paddington since the introduction of the full high-speed service in October 1976 and looks set to remain thus for several years to come. Seen on 20 March 1980 are power cars Nos 43132, 43033 and 43035, all of which were still working the services in 2007. *Gavin Morrison*

Right: Forming the down 'Bradford Executive' from King's Cross, set No 254 028 descends the 1-in-50 gradient from Laisterdyke to Bradford Interchange past Hammerton Street DMU depot on 15 May 1980. The site of the former Great Northern steam shed, latterly a DMU depot, is now occupied by a bus garage. *Gavin Morrison*

Left: Two power cars, from sets 254 009 and 254 013, pass Doncaster Carr depot on the East Coast main line on 26 March 1981, most likely heading for Bounds Green depot. *Gavin Morrison*

Below: The mighty Forth Bridge dwarfs the HST set working the down 'Aberdonian' — the 12.00 from King's Cross — as it approaches North Queensferry on its journey north on 12 April 1981. The difficult nature of the 13 miles from Edinburgh to Aberdeen gives the HSTs little opportunity to exploit their speed capabilities except between Dundee and Arbroath. *Gavin Morrison*

Below: An unidentified power car makes a smoky passage through Hunslet, on the southern outskirts of Leeds at the head of the 09.29 cross-country service from Leeds to Plymouth on 24 April 1983. The train had been diverted (due to engineering work) along the erstwhile Midland main line out of Leeds via Normanton Junction. *Gavin Morrison*

Right: Possibly the only occasion to date that a HST has travelled over Copy Pit Summit, on the ex-Lancashire & Yorkshire route through the Pennines between Todmorden and Burnley. On 25 September 1983 Western Region set No 253 028, with power cars Nos 43151 and 43126, and painted in the then new InterCity livery spent two days on the line for filming purposes, as at this time the route saw little traffic. Power car No 43151 is seen here on the rear at the summit. The filming was to have taken place on the Blackburn–Clitheroe–Hellifield line, until it was realised that Settle–Carlisle diversions would be in force on this weekend. *Gavin Morrison*

Left: In the days when cross-country services travelled between Sheffield Midland and York mainly via the Swinton and Knottingley line the 06.05 Bristol–Newcastle passes Broughton against the impressive backdrop of Ferrybridge power station's cooling towers on 17 April 1984. It is headed by No 43167, with No 43168 at the rear. The former was the first of four power cars to be fitted with a 2,400hp Mirrlees 12MB190 power unit, with which it re-entered service on 31 January 1987. The Mirrlees engines were fitted because of the excessive failures due to overheating with the Paxman units in the hot summer of 1983. Originally 140 were to have been installed, but in the event only four were actually fitted. *Gavin Morrison*

Right: The 16.42 Manchester Piccadilly–Plymouth approaches Stockport on 7 June 1984. The train comprises a Western Region set headed by No 43015, newly transferred to Laira depot after eight years at St Philip's Marsh, with No 43190 at the rear. In 2007 both power cars are still working West Country services. *Gavin Morrison*

Right: Until a few years ago when Virgin CrossCountry sets began working empty between Longsight and Neville Hill depots, the Trans-Pennine route via Standedge Tunnel hardly ever saw HSTs. One such occasion arose on 2 May 1985, when a set powered by Nos 43098 and 43154 worked a special press trip in connection with the launch of a new catering service. Painted in the then new InterCity livery, the train is shown approaching Diggle. *Gavin Morrison*

Left: An unidentified power car in the then new InterCity livery heads a set in the original livery out of Bristol Temple Meads towards Weston-super-Mare on 10 August 1985. In the background can be seen the rear of 'King'-class steam locomotive (No 6023 *King Edward II*) awaiting restoration, which 21 years later is nearing completion. *Gavin Morrison*

Below: Until the modernisation of the signalling in April 1986 Taunton was one of the best locations in the country for photographing impressive signal gantries. Here Nos 43034 and 43175 head west after passing the East signalbox and gantry on 22 August 1985. No 43034 was named *The Black Horse* in October 1994, but so far No 43175 remains one of the few power cars never to have carried a name. *Gavin Morrison*

Left: No 43185 brings up the rear of a Penzance-Paddington drawing into St Austell station on 6 September 1985 as Class 50 No 50 050 *Fearless* — the first of its class to be built in 1967 as No D400 but by now in 'large logo' livery — prepares to leave with a train for Penzance. No 43185 was named *Great Western* at Paddington in May 1992. *Gavin Morrison*

Below: A Class 56 can be seen outside 'The Plant' at Doncaster on 26 March 1986 as a morning express for King's Cross departs behind an unidentified power car. The latter is in the new InterCity livery, introduced in 1983, whilst the coaches are in the original blue and grey. *Gavin Morrison*

Left: Engineering work was taking place between Castle Cary and Exeter on 5 April 1986, so trains were diverted via Yeovil onto the ex-London & South Western main line to Exeter St Davids. Here an unidentified power car in InterCity livery, ostensibly from Western Region set No 253 040, brings up the rear of a six-coach train of blue-and-grey stock forming the 11.20 Penzance–Paddington as it descends the 1-in-80 gradient from Crewkerne Tunnel to Crewkerne station. *Gavin Morrison*

Right: No 43088 *XIII Commonwealth Games Scotland 1986* in original livery, but with a black number on the front, pulls away from Doncaster at the head of an express for King's Cross on 27 June 1986. It was named in a ceremony at Edinburgh Waverley station on 27 March 1985. *Gavin Morrison*

Left: On 28 June 1986 diversions affected services on the Midland main line. Here the 14.50 Nottingham–St Pancras passes Corby North headed by No 43060 *County of Leicestershire*, with No 43062 at the rear. At the time of writing (February 2007) No 43060 remains hard at work on the Midland main line, but No 43062 is now used by Network Rail to power the New Measurement Test Train. *Gavin Morrison*

Below left: Bound for Paddington on 2 March 1987, InterCity-liveried No 43032 (later named *The Royal Regiment of Wales*), passes Severn Tunnel Junction for Paddington with a train of original-liveried coaches and No 43034 at the rear. At this time Severn Tunnel Junction was a still busy freight centre with its own locomotive stabling-point, several Class 37s being visible in the background. *Gavin Morrison*

Right: New to the Western Region in April 1977, No 43049 was transferred to the Eastern Region after 5½ years and named *Neville Hill* in January 1984, since when it has been a favourite of that depot. This photograph shows it in the depot yard, being prepared for its next duty on 13 September 1987. It has been involved in two minor incidents at this depot, the first back in 1981 (at which time it was still based on the WR) and more recently in 2005; by great coincidence both also involved Trailer First No 41043. *Gavin Morrison*

Below: The 12.35 from Edinburgh Waverley to King's Cross, comprising stock in a mixture of liveries, passes the old Freightliner depot at Portobello, east of Edinburgh, on 16 September 1987. At its head is power car No 43116 *City of Kingston upon Hull*. Although its name was removed by GNER in January 1997 No 43116 remains at work on the East Coast main line in 2007. *Gavin Morrison*

Right: In InterCity days there were several variations in the colour schemes for the front of the cabs. Here power car No 43004, with yellow cab-window surrounds, leaves Sheffield at the head of an afternoon cross-country working on 14 May 1988. *Gavin Morrison*

Left: Diverted away from the Highland main line (at that time closed on Sunday mornings) via the old Great North of Scotland route to Aberdeen, the 'Highland Chieftain' from Inverness to King's Cross passes Insch on 25 September 1988. The leading power car, No 43041, was named *City of Discovery* at Dundee on 27 June 1990 but moved to the Western Region in 1991, having been displaced from the East Coast main line by Class 91 electrics. *Gavin Morrison*

Below: A line-up at the west end of Leeds City station on 18 February 1989, before the second rebuilding, includes No 43038 *National Railway Museum — The First 10 Years, 1975-1985*, which until May 1983 had been based on the Western Region. To the right can be seen a 'Pacer' diesel unit and an immaculate Class 47/4, No 47620 *Windsor Castle*, at that time the WR's Royal engine (and still extant today as No 47799 *Prince Henry*). In February 1991 No 43038 was fitted with new plates, these remaining *in situ* until March 1997; it was renamed by GNER in March 2002 as *The Royal Dragoon Guards* and again in November 2003 as *City of Dundee*, which moniker it retains in 2007. *Gavin Morrison*

Below: An HST set receives a wash at Kensal Green before moving to Old Oak Common depot for servicing on 6 May 1989. *Gavin Morrison*

Right: The 18.15 Aberdeen–Leeds accelerates away from Arbroath alongside the sea with power car No 43060 *County of Leicestershire* at the rear on 22 June 1989.

Allocated to the Western Region when new, this power car moved after a few months to Heaton but has spent most of its career to date on the Midland main line, where it is still working. The 15½ miles between Arbroath and Dundee of level and relatively straight track is the only stretch where the HSTs and 'Voyagers' can travel at 100mph between the Forth Bridge and Aberdeen. *Gavin Morrison*

Right: In the final InterCity 'swallow' livery No 43093, unnamed and with small front numbers, rounds the curve just south of the Tay Bridge at Wormit as it heads the 14.55 Aberdeen–King's Cross towards Edinburgh on 22 June 1989. Over the years it has been named *Yorkshire Post*, *Plymouth — Spirit of Discovery*, and after being displaced by Virgin 'Voyagers' on CrossCountry services, was named *Rio Triumph* by Midland Mainline. *Gavin Morrison*

Below: In the late 1980s there was a through HST working from King's Cross to Glasgow Queen Street, from where the unit worked back to Edinburgh Craigentinny for servicing. On 14 July 1989 No 43069 brings up the rear of a mismatched formation heading west past Glasgow's Eastfield depot. The line to the right links up with the West Highland line, while in the middle distance can be seen a Class 26 and a DMU in Strathclyde PTE livery. No 43069 later became a Virgin CrossCountry power car but after 'Voyagers' took over was transferred to Midland Mainline and named *Rio Enterprise. Gavin Morrison*

Right: Seen passing the site of Beeston station (closed 1 March 1953) on the southern outskirts of Leeds on 20 February 1990 is the 14.10 from Leeds to King's Cross, headed by No 43038, with a white cab roof and a full yellow end to its InterCity 'swallow' livery. Bringing up the rear was No 43198. *Gavin Morrison*

Below: A cross-country train, with power car No 43147 leading, glints in the late winter sunlight as it passes Clay Cross Junction and heads towards Derby on 10 January 1991. Just coming into view is Class 58 No 58033, heading north on a merry-go-round train. No 43147 was named *Red Cross* for nine years until 1997 but is currently unnamed. *Gavin Morrison*

Right: HSTs have seldom featured on enthusiast tours, but one notable exception occurred on 26 January 1991, when Hertfordshire Railtours chartered a set for an outing from St Pancras via Penistone and Healey Mills to Swinden Quarry, on the Grassington branch. No 43064 is shown about as close as it is possible to get to the buffer-stops in the quarry, while providing power at the other end was No 43076. The tour proved so successful that it was repeated the following weekend. *Gavin Morrison*

Heavy snow fell during the night on 8/9 February 1991, causing severe disruption to the following day's InterCity and Regional Railways services on the Midland main line. Here a late-running St Pancras–Sheffield express passes Clay Cross, with No 43120 leading and No 43039 at the rear. Both power cars had been allocated originally to the Western Region, until 1982 and 1983 respectively, and were based at Neville Hill until May 1998, when they passed to GNER at Craigentinny; No 43120 has since been fitted with an MTU 4000 power unit and renumbered 43320. *Gavin Morrison*

Another wintry scene on 12 December 1991 sees an express for St Pancras, headed by No 43075 and with No 43106 at the rear, passing the site of Kibworth station (closed in 1968). As late as 14.30 in the afternoon the frost was still clinging to the trees and grass. *Gavin Morrison*

Left: In 1987, pending the delivery of purpose-built Driving Van Trailers (DVTs) for use with the forthcoming Class 91 electric locomotives on the soon-to-be-electrified East Coast main line, it was decided that 10 HST power cars should be converted as 'surrogate DVTs' to enable trials to commence, initially with existing Class 86 electrics on the West Coast main line. Officially they were to become Driver Trailer Luggage Vans (numbered 82090-9), the original intention being that their diesel engines should be isolated, but in the event these remained operational. No 43123 was the first to emerge from Derby, in October, No 43014 following in November, and in 1988 a further six were converted at Stratford; ultimately only eight power cars were modified. After completion of the trials they settled down to normal HST work but retained conventional buffers, their most obvious distinguishing feature. Here, on 12 September 1992, No 43065 prepares to leave Bournemouth Central at the head of the 14.17 to Manchester Piccadilly. On the left of the picture can be seen a Class 442 EMU on a service from Waterloo. *Gavin Morrison*

Below: Two Western Region power cars — No 43018 leading and No 43125 at the rear — provide the power for the 08.53 Euston–Holyhead on 24 July 1993, seen passing one of the best-known locations on the North Wales main line at Penmaenmawr, with the Great Orme in the background. *Gavin Morrison*

Left: A sight now lost forever at St Pancras due to construction of the new Eurostar terminal. Three HST sets all in InterCity 'swallow' livery, line up to head north on the evening of 24 March 1994. The leading power cars are Nos 43082, 43060 and 43049, all of which at the time of writing (February 2007) are still working services on the Midland main line. *Gavin Morrison*

Below: Passing through the delightful scenery of the Cumbrian Fells in the Lune Gorge, an unidentified set heads north for Glasgow or Edinburgh with an afternoon Cross-Country working on 14 May 1994. *Gavin Morrison*

Below: The impressive Virgin Trains livery was unveiled at Edinburgh on 6 January 1997. In the new livery, complete with CrossCountry branding, No 43153 brings up the rear of the 06.57 Bristol–Newcastle just south of Moorthorpe on 23 April 1997. The line to the right led to Frickley Colliery, where around this time the last trains were removing coal before complete closure. *Gavin Morrison*

Inset: Virgin CrossCountry branding. 'XC' and 'cross country' were soon dropped. *Gavin Morrison*

Below: Freshly repainted in Virgin Trains livery with 'XC' branding, No 43068 *The Red Nose* heads a train of matching Mk 3 stock forming the daily Dundee–Penzance through working past Church Fenton on 3 May 1997. In November 2000 this power car was renamed *The Red Arrows*. *Gavin Morrison*

Right: GNER painted its trains and power cars in this dark-blue livery. Initially some had 'GNER' in off-white lettering, but all eventually had the standard gold letters. The trains are usually well cleaned and in the sun look quite impressive, but otherwise the livery is rather uninspiring, albeit somewhat enlivened recently through having the doors painted red. No 43039, later named *The Royal Dragoon Guards*, approaches Leeds past Wortley South on an early-morning working from King's Cross on 30 April 1997. *Gavin Morrison*

Way out ↗

Above: In 1997, when InterCity was considering a possible alteration to the livery for power cars dedicated to Euston–Holyhead/Blackpool services, a 'one-off' livery was applied to power car No 43028 by Longsight depot at Manchester. However, this variation apparently did not find favour with the authorities, and No 43028 ran in this condition for only a short time; here it is seen climbing out of Holyhead with the 13.52 to Euston on 2 August 1997. *Paul Corrie*

Left: The tide is fully in at picturesque Horse Cove as No 43190 brings up the rear of a Paddington-bound express on 16 August 1997. In the distance can be seen Dawlish and Langston Rock. The formation is in Great Western Trains livery with 'Merlin' logo, which regrettably would not last long following the FirstGroup takeover. *Gavin Morrison*

Right: Neville Hill depot at Leeds has had a very long association with the HSTs and is capable of carrying out major repairs. No 43082 receives a new cab on 11 September 1997. *Paul Corrie*

Left: In Great Western livery, with the 'Merlin' logo clearly visible on the bodyside, No 43191 *Sea Hawk* is bathed in gentle autumn sunlight as it races past Didcot East on 7 November 1997. Note the power station, clearly visible in the background. *Gavin Morrison*

Right: Midland Mainline, part of the National Express Group, came up with this very attractive and eye-catching livery, with 'MIDLAND MAINLINE' and stag logo on the side of the power car. Here No 43055 *Sheffield Star* heads an up afternoon Sheffield–St Pancras express through Hasland Cutting, south of Chesterfield, on 18 May 1998. *Gavin Morrison*

Below: On Sundays in 1998 the up 'Highland Chieftain' was timed to leave Inverness at 09.30 instead of the weekday time of 07.55. The train is seen on 24 May entering Carr Bridge on its 8½-hour journey to King's Cross behind No 43114 *East Riding of Yorkshire*, which until December 1996 had been named *National Garden Festival Gateshead 1990*. *Gavin Morrison*

Left: The driver of No 43019, in Great Western Trains 'Merlin' livery, gives the photographer a cheery wave as his train, an up express, passes the site of Aller Junction, just west of Newton Abbot, on 15 August 1998. This power car was destroyed in the tragic accident on the Berks & Hants line on 6 November 2004, when, travelling at 100mph, it hit a car that had stopped on the level crossing at Ufton Nervet, the impact derailing all coaches and the rear power car, resulting in seven deaths. *Gavin Morrison*

Below left: Sporting the Great Western 'Merlin' logo, No 43174 *Bristol–Bordeaux* heads a Swansea–Paddington express away from Newport and across the River Usk on 17 September 1998. In 2007 it is still employed on services out of Paddington. *Gavin Morrison*

Right: In recent years, to provide Summer Saturday extras from the North of England to Newquay, Virgin CrossCountry has hired additional HST sets from GNER and, as here, Midland Mainline. Seen from Langston Rock, power car No 43050 heads west towards Dawlish with the 1V38 06.05 Leeds–Newquay on 19 July 1998. *Gavin Morrison*

Below: The Midland Mainline sets that are serviced overnight at Leeds Neville Hill depot form three early-morning services from Leeds to St Pancras. Headed by No 43052 and with No 43051 at the rear, the Saturday 07.55 to St Pancras crosses the embankment near Leeds United FC's Elland Road stadium on 1 May 1999. *Gavin Morrison*

Right: Another set in GWT's 'Merlin' livery, headed by power car No 43033, races past Slough towards Paddington at around 125mph on 3 July 1999. No 43033 has since been named *Driver Brian Cooper 15th June 1947 – 5th October 1999*. *Gavin Morrison*

Below: Headed by No 43089, the 09.11 Newcastle–Birmingham nears the end of its journey as it passes the Motorail sidings at Washwood Heath on 11 July 1999. Having entered service on the Eastern Region in June 1978, No 43089 was transferred in February 1982 to Plymouth Laira, where it spent much of its time on cross-country work; it was to remain with the Virgin CrossCountry franchise until replaced by 'Voyagers', thereafter being employed on St Pancras–Manchester 'Project Rio' services in Midland Mainline livery. *Gavin Morrison*

Right: A line-up of different liveries at Glasgow Central on 12 August 1999. On the left of the picture is one of the eight buffer-fitted power cars, No 43123, ready to head south with a Virgin CrossCountry service; stabled on the centre road is Strathclyde EMU No 303 058, while on the right is a GNER DVT at the rear of an express from King's Cross. *Gavin Morrison*

Right: When Great Western Trains was taken over by FirstGroup its livery was modified by the addition of a gold band and the replacement of the GWT 'Merlin' logo by First's corporate *'f'*. Reflecting these changes, No 43004 *Borough of Swindon* stands at Newport, having arrived with an express for Swansea on 1 October 1999. Having emerged from Crewe Works in March 1976, it was paired with No 43008 for trials around Newcastle before settling down that September to service on the Great Western main line, where it currently remains. In 2005, in common with No 43009 it was fitted experimentally with an MTU 16V4000 power unit, and plans now are in hand to fit the remainder of Angel Trains' HST power cars with this type of engine. *Gavin Morrison*

Left: Another set in First Great Western livery passes St Brides with an up express on the almost entirely level four-track section of line between Cardiff and Newport on 2 October 1999. *Gavin Morrison*

Below: A GNER set headed by No 43116 (until January 1997 named *City of Kingston upon Hull*) passes the now closed (and in 2007 soon to be demolished) Gascoigne Wood pit on the frosty morning of 28 December 1999, when, due to engineering work at Leeds, GNER was using HSTs to provide a shuttle service to/from Doncaster via the Hambleton Curve. *Gavin Morrison*

Still with Virgin 'XC' branding, No 43093 *Lady in Red* heads the 09.10
Aberdeen–Plymouth past Saughton Junction — to the west of Edinburgh,
where the Glasgow and Aberdeen lines part company — on 21 February 2000.
Until January 1997 named *York Festival*, this power car is one of 12 purchased
by First Great Western from Porterbrook Leasing in October 2004 and is currently
fitted with an MTU 16V4000 power unit. *Gavin Morrison*

Below: In June 1998 power car No 43101 (until the previous month named *Edinburgh International Festival*) received the name *The Irish Mail*, not in the form of a conventional nameplate but by the application of a vinyl sticker, and is seen thus adorned passing Winwick, north of Warrington, on a down working on 4 March 2000. Similar stickers were used to name Nos 43100 *Blackpool Rock* and 43157 *HMS Penzance* (as well as a Class 90 electric locomotive), but fortunately their use was discontinued following the appointment of Chris Green as Chief Executive of Virgin Trains. No 43101 is currently (2007) out of use at the Brush works. *Gavin Morrison*

Right: An HST set in full First Great Western livery draws into Exeter St Davids with an express for the West Country on 7 August 2000. In the past Western Region expresses normally used the platforms to the far right, but nowadays Platforms 4 and 5 are the norm. *Gavin Morrison*

On a cold and frosty 30 December 2000 a diverted Virgin CrossCountry express headed by No 43156, with No 43008 at the rear, passes Burton Salmon *en route* from York to Leeds, where it will have to reverse before continuing its journey south. The diversion was necessitated by engineering work to the west of Church Fenton. *Gavin Morrison*

During the early part of 2001 the Vale of York experienced severe flooding, which caused extensive damage to property. This picture, taken at Rythir, on the East Coast main line, shows the results of the River Ouse bursting its banks; under normal conditions the river's course takes it past the houses in the background. Aided by No 43106 at the rear, No 43109 has just crossed the river bridge with the morning Aberdeen–King's Cross on 12 February 2001. *Gavin Morrison*

HST workings over the Trans-Pennine Standedge route were extremely rare until Neville Hill and Longsight depots started to maintain sets for Virgin CrossCountry, and empty stock workings (ECS) between the two sites took place, occasionally during daylight. Seen on Sunday 2 June 2001 is one such working, the 09.30 Neville Hill–Longsight, headed by one of the buffer-fitted power cars, No 43123, with No 43092 at the rear. This picture was taken from the A62 road above the entrance to Standedge Tunnel at Marsden. The canal basin is on the left, the tunnel to the bottom left of the picture. *Gavin Morrison*

Headed by power car No 43188 *City of Plymouth* in First Great Western livery, the down 'Cornish Riviera Express' heads west past the graveyard at Powderham Church on 27 July 2001. The gravestone is in memory of Elizabeth Bale, who died in 1914. *Gavin Morrison*

A Virgin CrossCountry service for Bournemouth arrives at Birmingham International behind No 43098 *The Railway Children* on 28 September 2001. Between September 1984 and December 1987 this power car had carried the name *Tyne & Wear Metropolitan County. Gavin Morrison*

With No 43069 bringing up the rear, the 11.20 Glasgow Central–Plymouth draws into Crewe station on 29 March 2002. No 43069 entered service in December 1977 on the Eastern Region, where it remained until moving to Plymouth Laira in May 1998 as part of the Virgin CrossCountry fleet; displaced by the introduction of 'Voyagers', it was transferred in 2003 to Midland Mainline for use on 'Project Rio' services, duly receiving that company's blue livery. *Gavin Morrison*

Below: The initial version of FirstGroup corporate livery for the HST power cars included a white flash on the cabside. No 43023 heads west past Teignmouth boatyard with an almost uniform rake of stock on 3 April 2002. This style of livery was soon replaced by all blue, with just a flash of pink to break up the bodyside. *Paul Corrie*

Right: This book would not be complete without a photograph of power car No 43008, seen ready to leave Carlisle with the 07.19 Penzance–Glasgow on 1 May 2002. It entered service in October 1976. By 2001 it had achieved the highest mileage of any power car, having covered eight million miles in 25 years' service. Putting this into perspective, a few of the Gresley 'A3' Pacifics managed just over two million in 40 years. It has served many different operators — InterCity, Great Western, First Great Western, Virgin CrossCountry and, currently, GNER, carrying the name *City of Aberdeen* — and is no doubt well on its way to nine million. *Gavin Morrison*

Left: On 23 May 2002 the normal route between Sheffield and Wakefield was closed for engineering works, so services were diverted by Barnsley and Normanton. No 43090 brings up the rear of the Virgin CrossCountry 11.50 Poole–Edinburgh as it passes Barnsley in fantastic lighting conditions which lasted for at least an hour, when all around was getting soaked!
Gavin Morrison

Below: Buffer-fitted No 43014 emerges from beneath the canopy of Chester General station as it leaves with the 13.35 Holyhead–Euston on 14 September 2002. Its career with Virgin over, it was transferred to Network Rail and painted in yellow livery for working the New Measurement Train.
Gavin Morrison

Right: The 09.46 Penzance–Paddington is only 13 miles into its journey as it passes through Camborne station on 23 November 2002. Leading power car No 43003 is in the then new FirstGroup livery, which has since been superseded, the white area being replaced by more blue, with gold numbers. *Gavin Morrison*

Below: The 10.41 Penzance–Paddington headed by No 43040 in the initial version of FirstGroup's smart, predominantly blue livery, passes the site of Marazion station, which closed on 5 October 1964, and was well-known for the camping coaches located there; a derelict Pullman Car can be seen to the left of this picture taken on 23 November 2002. New to the Western Region in December 1976, No 43040 worked on the Eastern Region from May 1983 before returning to the Western in September 1990; in the meantime, in a ceremony held at Aberdeen on 27 June 1990, it received the name *Granite City*, which it retained until January 1996. *Gavin Morrison*

Left: Rendered surplus to requirements at Virgin CrossCountry, power car No 43062 is one of three used by Network Rail for powering the New Measurement Train, used to assess the condition of track. Fresh from overhaul at Neville Hill, it is seen in the depot yard on 25 January 2003 before entering service in its new role. *Gavin Morrison*

Right: Replaced by 'Voyagers' on Virgin CrossCountry workings, No 43184 moved to Midland Mainline. Put to work immediately, it initially retained red livery minus Virgin logos, in which condition it is seen passing Wellingborough at the rear of the 13.27 Sheffield–St Pancras on 20 February 2003. One of four power cars owned by Angel Trains that are currently in use with Midland Mainline, it has since received that operator's later blue livery. *Gavin Morrison*

Below: Two power cars side-by-side at Neville Hill, Leeds, on 2 March 2003. On the left is No 43088 in Virgin colours, on the right No 43166, the first to be painted in the new Midland Mainline livery. No 43088 has since moved on to First Great Western and has received FirstGroup livery. *Gavin Morrison*

Left: The 08.40 Euston–Holyhead heads north past Leighton Buzzard and approaches Linslade Tunnel on 24 June 2003. Headed by power car No 43092 *Institution of Mechanical Engineers 150th Anniversary 1847-1997*, with No 43160 at the rear, the train will arrive at Holyhead in time to meet the morning ferries from Dun Laoghaire, the return journey to Euston departing at 13.35. *Gavin Morrison*

Below: To compensate for the disruption to services caused by the upgrading of the West Coast main line the Strategic Rail Authority authorised an hourly service between Manchester and St Pancras, under a scheme known as 'Project Rio'.

The HST power cars and sets used thereon were mainly ex Virgin CrossCountry, but for a time two power cars and a set of coaches were hired from First Great Western. Perhaps inevitably the power cars and set got parted, which helps to explain why on 23 September 2003 the 14.47 Manchester Piccadilly–St Pancras, seen between Chinley station and Chinley Junction, included no fewer than *four* different liveries; behind power car No 43009 in First livery are a coach in the new Midland Mainline scheme, six coaches in Virgin red and power car No 43073 in the old Midland Mainline colours! *Gavin Morrison*

In recent years the view of the viaduct over the River Aln, just to the north of Alnmouth, has become increasingly obscured by trees, but before the leaves appear it is possible to see a little more of the structure. Here the 12.00 King's Cross–Inverness, in the latest GNER livery (with red carriage doors) and headed by No 43119 *Harrogate Spa*, crosses on 17 March 2004. *Gavin Morrison*

The 'Project Rio' service between Manchester and St Pancras provided excellent photographic opportunities in the Hope Valley, which normally sees only diesel multiple-units and a few freights. The 12.00 St Pancras–Manchester is shown climbing Normans Bank (near Edale) on 18 May 2004, its eight trailer coaches, in the latest Midland Mainline colours, 'topped and tailed' by power cars 43052 and 43044 in that operator's earlier livery. *Gavin Morrison*

Left: On the last day of HST workings on Euston–Holyhead services, 21 May 2004, the 08.40 from Euston was headed by buffer-fitted power car No 43080, which, most unusually, was allowed to carry an appropriate headboard. No 43080 is shown, minus Virgin decals, inside the trainshed at Holyhead. The other power car was No 43065 — also a buffer-fitted example, so that the headboard could be carried on the return working. *Gavin Morrison*

Below: The 18.01 departure from Derby to St Pancras on 14 June 2004 sets off round the sharp left-hand curve behind No 43058, newly repainted in the latest Midland Mainline livery. This power car was given the name *Midland Pride* in February 1997 but lost this upon repaint. *Gavin Morrison*

Below: The St Pancras–Manchester 'Project Rio' services were routed via the Erewash Valley, which provided the opportunity to photograph regular passenger workings passing Toton Yard. Here two ex-Virgin CrossCountry power cars, suitably repainted, provide the power for the 13.47 from Manchester Piccadilly on 1 September 2004. Both were named, No 43159 (leading) as *Rio Warrior* and No 43087 as *Rio Invader*. The lines in the foreground lead to the locomotive depot. *Gavin Morrison*

Right: Retaining its *City of Aberdeen* nameplates and red livery but minus its Virgin decals, No 43155 arrives at Manchester Piccadilly at the rear of a rake of ex-Virgin coaches forming the 12.00 Midland Mainline 'Project Rio' service on 7 September 2004. *Gavin Morrison*

Below: A brilliantly clear day, 14 September 2004, provides another view of the 12.00 King's Cross–Inverness, this time headed by No 43105 *City of Inverness* and racing north along the scenic coastline at Spittal, near Tweedmouth, before crossing the Royal Border Bridge at Berwick. *Gavin Morrison*

Right: Headed by an unidentified power car, a set in GNER's usual immaculate external condition and with red doors on the coaches races through Drem station on the 07.55 Aberdeen–King's Cross, 15 September 2004. *Gavin Morrison*

By 19 February 2005 virtually all the Midland Mainline coaches had received the new livery, although many of the power cars had still to be repainted. Against the backdrop of the famous Brush Falcon Works, No 43055 *Sheffield Star*, fitted with a Paxman 12VP185 engine, heads north with the 13.45 St Pancras–Sheffield. *Gavin Morrison*

Right: Headed by power car No 43062, Network Rail's high-speed New Measurement Train passes through the closed station of Brightside, just north of Sheffield, on the Saturday-morning 08.59 Etches Park–Craigentinny working on 7 May 2005. *Gavin Morrison*

Below: Another view of Network Rail's New Measurement Train, here travelling at line speed past Carpenders Park, south of Watford, on the 15.30 diagram from Crewe to Euston on 8 June 2005. No 43062 is shown on the rear. The five-coach train consists of rebuilt Mk 3 stock, except for car No 999550, which was a purpose-built Mk 2 test car. *Gavin Morrison*

Left: In the original Midland Mainline livery, No 43060 *County of Leicestershire* rushes south past Wellingborough at the head of the 10.30 Nottingham–St Pancras, with No 43046 at the rear, on 30 August 2005. By this date very few power cars were still in this livery, and all the coaches had been repainted. Midland Mainline has decided that only two of its power cars will retain names, these being Nos 43049 *Neville Hill* and 43072 *Derby Etches Park*. *Gavin Morrison*

Below: Headed by power car No 43057 in the latest Midland Mainline livery and comprising a rake of matching stock, the 09.55 St Pancras–Nottingham rushes non-stop past Wellingborough on 30 August 2005. Regrettably the overall effect is somewhat compromised by the second power car, which is still in the earlier Midland Mainline colours. *Gavin Morrison*

Left: An express for Paddington passes South Moreton, east of Didcot, on 17 August 2005, both power cars — Nos 43031 (leading) and 43189 — being in the revised version of First corporate livery. *Gavin Morrison*

Below: Glorious sunshine along the sea wall at Dawlish on 21 November 2005. No 43185 *Great Western* brings up the rear of the 09.45 Plymouth–Paddington as Class 150/2 DMU No 150266, in Wessex Trains' distinctive livery, heads west as the 09.54 Exmouth–Paignton. *Gavin Morrison*

Below: The number of pictures taken at Cockwood Harbour must run to thousands if not millions. Here, on 21 November 2005, No 43183 heads the 10.30 Paddington–Plymouth as Class 220 'Voyager' No 220006 *Clyde Voyager* disappears out of the picture on the 13.25 Plymouth–Glasgow Central. *Gavin Morrison*

Right: In the early months of 2006 Virgin CrossCountry hired a spare Midland Mainline set to work the 1V29 07.05 Leeds–Plymouth and return to help with shortages of 'Voyagers' and also to enable its crews to retain traction knowledge on HSTs. At the familiar location of Langston Rock No 43057 and its train, all in the latest Midland Mainline livery, head west on 6 March 2006. *Gavin Morrison*

No 43004 *First for the future / First ar gyfer y dyfodol* pauses at Newton Abbot at the head of the 1Z30 09.12 Paddington–Penzance special to launch the renewed Great Western franchise on 3 April 2006. The train, which ran via Swindon, Bristol, Weston-super-Mare and Exeter, comprised three re-liveried coaches (TGS 44049, TRFB 40752 and TF 41003) and power car No 43009 at the rear, both power cars being fitted with MTU engines. The 'Dynamic Lines' livery has since been dropped for power cars but is retained (albeit in revised form) for carriage stock.
Robert Pritchard

Right: On Sundays in the spring of 2006, due to engineering work south of Leeds on the Doncaster line, GNER services to London were worked by HST sets and diverted via Micklefield and the Hambleton Curve. Here, on 30 April 2006, No 43112 *Doncaster* passes the now closed Gascoigne Wood pit (which was already being dismantled) with the 12.38 departure from Leeds, which it would work only as far as Finsbury Park, as a result of more engineering work around King's Cross.
Gavin Morrison

Left: Power car No 43070, painted in Cotswold Rail livery, trundles slowly past the site of the old Rotherham Masborough station on 27 May 2006. An excursion, the 1Z27 07.10 Dursley–Scarborough, the train comprises Midland Mainline coaches, while at the rear is power car No 43087 in red Hornby advertising livery. *Gavin Morrison*

Below left: A brief signal check allowed a second picture of No 43070 from the other side of the bridge at Rotherham Masborough. Displaced by 'Voyagers' from Virgin CrossCountry services, it passed to Midland Mainline for use on 'Project Rio' services; when these finished it was sent (along with No 43069) for exhibition at the National Railway Museum, York. During 2005 it was taken over by Cotswold Rail for use on special workings but is currently (February 2007) out of use at Plymouth Laira depot. *Gavin Morrison*

Right and below: Bringing up the rear of the Dursley–Scarborough special of 27 May 2006, Hornby-liveried No 43087 is shown in the cutting just to the north of Rotherham Masborough station, restarting from the signal check. This was another power car to pass to Cotswold Rail following the cessation of 'Project Rio' services. Like No 43070 it is currently languishing out of use at Plymouth Laira, where it is yielding spare parts; both power cars are expected ultimately to be fitted with MTU engines and re-enter service with First Great Western. *Gavin Morrison*

Right: No 43049 *Neville Hill* — one of only two Midland Mainline power cars currently named — heads the 13.25 St Pancras–Sheffield past Cossington (between Leicester and Barrow-on-Soar) on 6 June 2006.

Left: Formed by a typically immaculate GNER set, the 09.55 from Aberdeen to King's Cross passes the annual Highland Games as it slows for the curves at Burntisland, Fife, on 17 July 2006. The train is headed by No 43008, which earlier in its post-BR career had worked for Great Western and Virgin Trains. *Gavin Morrison*

Below: In the latest First Great Western livery No 43026 heads the 13.30 Paddington–Bristol Temple Meads past Denchworth (just to the west of Wantage) on 16 December 2006. *John Turner*

Left: It was hoped that BR's High Speed Train would generate significant export orders, but in the event the only such order came from New South Wales in Australia, for 26 power cars, 66 stainless-steel trailer cars and eight driving trailers. Somewhat different in appearance from their British counterparts, these trains were introduced in 1982. In the very striking XPT livery power car No XP2008 *City of Goulburn* stands in Melbourne's Spencer Street station — a first visit for the type — in November 1990. *F. Bullock*

Right: The original power car, No XP2000, originally named *City of Maitland*, was painted into this striking blue livery to promote the Olympic Games to be held in Sydney in 2000. It is seen at Wagga Wagga, New South Wales, on a Sydney–Melbourne service in January 1997. *F. Bullock*

Below: In a distinctive two tone blue livery a 'Countrylink' set on a Sydney–Melbourne express enters Benalla, Victoria, in January 1997. *F. Bullock*

In conclusion, an unidentified power car and train, seen in the original attractive BR livery, is powering up the 1 in 100 from Sheffield Midland to Bradway tunnel with an up express on 13 August 1983. *Gavin Morrison*